NETWORKING FOR AUTHORS

*How to Build Your Fan Base and
Book Sales through Networking*

Heidi Thorne

Thorne Communications LLC

ISBN: 9798609753014

Thorne Communications LLC, USA, www.HeidiThorne.com

CONTENTS

INTRODUCTION: YOU SHOULD BE NETWORKING

I have to laugh when I see vague or even misguided suggestions that authors should do networking. But what does that mean?

Networking is the process of building your tribe of colleagues, customers, and fans that follow and support your work. In the publishing arena, this is often referred to as your author platform or fan base. These are people who are glad to consume, buy, and share your work because you provide them value.

If you're an author who has written books as a private side hustle or hobby, you may be scared to go to networking events and publicly declare that you're an author. Even if you've been in business working for yourself or a company, networking for your author business is something completely different. Whichever situation describes you, understanding the networking game can help build your author fan base and your book sales.

But where and how do you start building your author network? I'll answer this burning question for you by sharing what I've experienced and observed.

Why My Networking Was Not Working When I Became An Author

I had been in sales, advertising, and publishing for decades. I had a reputation of being very visible and recognized in my local business and industry networking scene.

But then I shifted gears to concentrate on my writing career. Almost instantly I was irrelevant to most of the network I had spent years building, and they were irrelevant to me. This wasn't just for in-person networking. It happened on social media, too. And my list of email subscribers? Well, that went to almost zero with my new direction. Back to square one with network and fan base building.

With a large share of my existing network out of the picture, I tried going to Meetup group events. Met some nice people, but just not the people, or enough of the people, I needed to meet.

My focus for social media shifted as well. Twitter used to be my primary network for years. Now I had to pay more attention to Facebook, and Instagram, too, which is a challenge with the non-visual nature of my topic and work. LinkedIn, which you would think would be ideal for my business-focused writing and editing services, surprisingly just wasn't (and currently isn't) driving anything significant.

So what should you understand from my story? Realize that your author fan base and network could be a completely different group of folks from your existing tribe of family, friends, customers, and colleagues. You're also always in fan base building mode from here forward. And your network building efforts may need to change quickly and dramatically in response to changes in how your fans and social media behave.

CHAPTER 1: WHO IS YOUR IDEAL READER?

Figuring out how to connect with people who will read and buy your books and follow you starts with identifying who your fans are and who you are.

I am always shocked when new author clients don't know who ideal readers are for their books. Typically, they try to convince me that their books are for "everyone." That is never true. Or they'll identify such a broad audience for their books that it would be impossible to market. For example, I've had authors say their books are for women. Okay, well that narrows it down to about 50 percent of the world's population. My sarcasm should be obvious.

Before you even start networking to promote your book, you better know the following about your potential readers for your book. Note that if you write books for children, your book buyer is really the parent, maybe a grandparent or other adult gift giver. So determine the following for the adult buyer, not the child.

- Age.
- Gender and/or sexual orientation.

- Education level.

- Reading level. If you write children's books, adult buyers especially want to know if your book is appropriate for the reading grade level of the child who will receive the book. But reading level is a concern for adult books, too, if your book requires a college or specialized education to understand.

- What they do all day. Be specific.

- Hobbies or interests.

- Religious or philosophical beliefs, or experiences, that impact their attitudes and views of the world.

- Expectations from buying and reading your book. Your book must deliver on at least one of these E-values: entertainment, education, enlightenment, or encouragement. Entertainment gives them enjoyment or escapism. Education offers helpful information to enable them to build new skills. Enlightenment can help them think differently or more clearly. Encouragement can help them feel better about themselves and their lives.

This creates an ideal reader profile. Once you have the profile, you can search for networking groups, events, and online communities where you are more likely to encounter people that fit this profile. But you're not ready to start looking for groups of potential fans and connections just yet. There's one more important person you need to identify which we'll discuss next.

CHAPTER 2: WHO ARE YOU?

Surprised that I started out suggesting you figure out who your reader is? That was intentional. Now you need to figure out who you are and how you connect with that ideal reader.

You'll be determining the same things about yourself that you did for your readers.

- Age.

- Gender and/or sexual orientation.

- Education level.

- What you do all day. Be specific.

- Hobbies or interests.

- Religious or philosophical beliefs, or experiences, that impact your attitudes and view of the world.

How are your demographics the same or different than those of your readers and buyers? If they are dramatically different, why do you feel you can connect with them through your book?

Most of the author clients I've had are pretty similar to their readers in terms of their tastes, interests, and demographics. In fact, the desire to reach and serve an audience similar to themselves is why many of them feel compelled to write a book in the first place.

Even if they're different than their readers, some authors are experts at attracting and serving certain audiences. Maybe they worked with people like their readers in their careers, or have some other special understanding and experience with this group. Their books become an extension and expansion of those connections.

But occasionally there are authors who have wild and fantastical notions about the readers they want to reach. And their books show their ignorance of their readers' wants, needs, and preferences. If you are not part of your reader community or have no expertise in serving them, you could have a difficult time recruiting new fans. These people will sniff you out as a poser and an outsider not worthy of their attention. You might even offend some of them.

You might be thinking, *"What does it matter that I personally am similar to, or can relate to my readers? Shouldn't my book be the reason readers buy?"* Readers buy the book, as well as what and who the author is. You and your work are inseparable in most readers' minds. If the two of you are incongruent, you will be seen as inauthentic and lacking in integrity. Know who you are. Be who you are. And let your books be a reflection of you.

Introvert Or Extrovert?

In addition to the qualities you've just identified about yourself, would you say that you're more introverted or extroverted?

Many people think that authors are introverted, slaving

away in solitude and silence. Well, that might be true for some authors. But I know a lot of extroverted ones, too. Networking as an author is hard for both types. Here's why.

Introverts

You can't be a hermit and hope to have fans for your work. So the common advice to introverted authors is "get out of the house and meet people." I'm not quick to spew that advice, especially now when making connections with fans is easier and more efficient than it's ever been because of the internet and social media. No in-person meetings required. But you still need to build your author brand, even if it's just on social media or somewhere online.

Extroverts

Surprised that extrovert authors can find networking challenging? True, if you drop them into a physical room full of people, or plop them into an active online group, they'll get up to speed quickly on a social level.

But on a book level, extroverted authors can come across as too overly promotional, pushy, and have to constantly monitor themselves. It's like once they become authors, a switch gets flipped and they start burning relationship bridges. They can easily slip into "buy my book" or "in my book I talk about…" mode too often, making others feel uncomfortable. Instead of wanting more information on the author's book, people will want to get away from these authors as quickly as possible. Online, book hawkers get unfollowed and ignored.

The usual advice I give to all small businesses and authors is to limit your promotional messages to about 10 percent of your total posts or marketing emails. That's tolerable for most people, but still gets your word out.

How Do You Network If You Use A Pen Name?

Here's something most business people don't have to deal with when networking: How do you introduce yourself if you use a pen name, or pseudonym? What if you have multiple pseudonyms?

Authors often want to stretch their writing capabilities by diving into other genres or even different topics within their regular genre. That's not a problem in theory, and it can expand your audience, book sales opportunities, and the fulfillment you get from writing.

But you have to be realistic if you decide to expand into these new writing horizons under a pen name or names. In today's hyperconnected internet world, keeping your real identity a secret can be challenging, in spite of best efforts. The following example illustrates how a reveal of your alternate writing identity can impact your writing career.

I read a story in the publishing news about an author of YA (young adult) fiction who was invited to speak at a YA book conference. But then the conference learned that she also wrote and published erotica for adults under a pen name. She was then disinvited as a speaker because the conference felt that having her there would be in conflict with the YA market. Ouch! Now, how will the YA market respond to her work in the future?

When you register to join a networking group or event, you'll probably use your own real contact and payment information. So the event or group organizer could know who you are for real. They should keep that confidential.

But these things have the possibility of slipping out at some point along the way, even if you tell event organizers to use your pen name. You also could bump into people at in-person events, or even online, who know who you really are. They could blow your cover instantly!

So what should you do?

Decide if this new genre is worth the effort. This is a pretty big strategic decision for your self publishing career. I totally understand that you want to stretch your writing limits. But by doing so, and if your real identity gets revealed, will you be alienating your primary fan base that you've worked so hard to build? If your additional new genre has potential to put off your fans, then carefully weigh if you're willing to take the risk. If the new genre would not be offensive to most of your fans, then it's probably not a problem to consider new writing territory, whether under your regular author name or a pen name.

Consider owning up to the pen name if appropriate. One popular author clearly tells her followers what she publishes under each author identity. She publishes nonfiction under her real name, but then puts her fiction work under a separate pseudonym. If your primary fan base wouldn't be offended by your new genre adventures, or if you think they'd be interested in your other work, you could let them know about your new works and where to find them under your other author identity.

Make sure you have an author page on Amazon, website, and social media profiles for each identity. If you are trying to keep your work in each genre separate, then it is absolutely essential to have a separate author page on Amazon for each identity. You can set up multiple author pages through Author Central. Also set up a separate website and social media profiles for each identity. When you network, tell interested folks to visit the appropriate sites or profiles for the pen name you're promoting to help prevent confusion.

Pick and stick with a primary author identity that you'll use in each networking scenario, whether in person or online. Don't confuse your fans by using multiple identities in the same networking group or event. Don't use one pen name this month, then another pen name next month. Trying to keep track of what identities you're using and where you're using them can be confusing for you, too.

Be prepared to handle a reveal of your pen name. As in the example discussed earlier, your alternate genre identity always carries the risk of being revealed. How do you plan to handle that? Your work will already be out in the world and you can't take it back. Actually, this should be your first consideration before you even publish something under a pen name.

Is this all sounding like a lot of work and potential expense? It is. So carefully consider whether it's worth establishing a pen name.

CHAPTER 3: WHERE TO NETWORK

The biggest challenge to author networking is finding places to network. Most of the standard networking groups have little relevance or potential for authors. Here are some of the most common networking opportunities.

Chambers Of Commerce And Business Leads Groups

Chambers of commerce, leads groups (such as BNI and LeTip), and other standard in-person business networking events just aren't where author connections are plentiful or fruitful.

It's not that these groups are bad. They just don't usually provide an ideal mix of attendees for authors, even for most business authors. The attendees are those who want to meet customers and referral partners for their B2B (business to business) or B2C (business to consumer) businesses. That's not most authors, especially those that write fiction.

One of the other things about these groups is that regular participation is either suggested or required. That could mean monthly, bi-weekly, or even weekly meetings.

In leads groups, members are often expected to bring new business leads and referrals to every meeting, even if those meetings are every week. As a former president of a BNI networking chapter, I can tell you that this is very challenging, even if you're an active business. For an author, it can be an impossible task.

On top of the expense of energy it would take to be an active member, there may be hard dollar expenses, too, that could run into the hundreds or thousands of dollars in membership or meeting fees every year. This would wipe out any money you'd make from book sales to these groups.

Meetup Groups

Meetup is a website and mobile app that facilitates and promotes in-person local meetings for all sorts of interests. Some are useful, many are not, especially when it comes to author networking.

My experience with Meetup groups for my books and even other networking has been mixed. I found a large and active group that had potential for both my books and editing services. But I needed to attend and participate regularly to establish awareness and make connections. So I had to spend a fair amount of time (and money) to gain any results. Most other groups were too small or irrelevant to produce any significant results.

If you are trying to gain an understanding of a particular interest group, Meetups can be a good way to gather intel on concerns and attitudes for your market, maybe just not sales.

Before you expend too much energy and time in Meetup type groups, check out the profiles of who's in the group. Unfortunately, many Meetup users are vague and don't even completely fill out their profiles. Lazy? Scared? Have nothing to offer? All of the above? Whatever the reason, you might have to visit the group to get a better idea of the potential the group offers, or the lack of it. Even if the Meetup group is free or just a few dollars to attend, the amount of time, travel, and energy you might have to expend to explore and evaluate the group could be significant.

You'll also notice that once you establish a profile on Meetup, you'll get a flood of notices that this or that new group has just started up related to the interests you've chosen. This is helpful for you to monitor new author networking opportunities. Be aware, though, that Meetup groups come and go. This is primarily because Meetup typically gives event organizers a free trial period to get their groups going. Then when organizers realize how much of an investment it is in dollars, time, and energy, the group can fizzle out when the free trial ends.

Book Clubs

When people hear I'm an author, I sometimes get the suggestion that book clubs are probably great for networking. That's not the case for me as a business nonfiction author. But for fiction, they could be an opportunity if you understand the following for either offline or online clubs.

If you attend book club meetings, even as an author, you'll probably be expected to participate in the discussions. You can't just drop in, announce" I wrote a book," and hope club members will be thrilled that you've graced them with your presence. And if you're only there to promote your book, then be gone, you'll be branded as self-serving.

Understand the rules and etiquette before you pitch your book for a group's reading assignment. A leader, an influential member, or a member group vote may choose the books for the club to read. There may also be attendance and participation rules to follow.

If your book does become a featured read for the club, you have to determine how much you'll need or want to participate in the discussions. You may be setting yourself up for some arguments with members over parts of your books, too. Are you ready for that without becoming defensive of your work?

There are book club directories online for both offline and online groups. Some book clubs are using Meetup. Local libraries, churches, park districts, schools, and other community organizations may have book clubs. Opportunities will depend on what's available in your area.

Goodreads And Book Recommendation Sites

On a related note to book clubs, Goodreads has been noted as a good place for authors to connect with readers. For those of you who are not familiar, Goodreads is a book recommendation site where readers virtually gather to discover, discuss, and review books. It is now owned by Amazon.

In theory, it sounds like a great idea. For some genres and audiences, it might be. But for others, not so much.

I have intentionally ignored Goodreads because my business nonfiction market isn't really hanging out there. The only way you can figure out if it's for you and your work is to go there and check it out.

These recommendation sites may also have paid advertising and promotion opportunities for authors. Usually that means that authors pay a fee to provide their books for free to readers to help build awareness and possibly reviews. My impression from authors who have used these services is that many readers love getting free books that these promotions provide, but rarely does this translate into more sales, Amazon reviews, or new true fans. Be careful, too, that the site you're considering isn't a paid book review site. That could get you in trouble with Amazon for using them. Not worth the risk.

I also think that book recommendation sites don't really have the same clout as they did in the pre-Amazon era. Readers can now go directly to Amazon or other book retail sites or social media to find reviews prior to buying. That's what I do as a reader. Don't you?

Facebook Groups And Online Communities

Facebook Groups can foster authentic connections and conversations. I will say that many of the groups I've joined have become great discussion platforms and provide me with a lot of market intel. I even lead my own Facebook Group.

Facebook Groups can be networking at its easiest. No meetings to attend, unless the admin leaders host an event online or offline. Currently, they're free to join and participate, although some groups have paid off-Facebook membership requirements before you're allowed to join. In those cases, the Group is really just a place for an organization's members to communicate.

You may also be able to find book discussion forums in online communities such as Quora. However, conversations and connections on these forums may be short lived, dissolving once a focused discussion concludes.

As on Meetup, Facebook Group and online community quality and activity levels vary widely, so check out several. Plan to actively participate in groups that discuss your book's topic or genre. Share useful articles. Thoughtfully comment on posts and share your insight and experience to help others. Don't be a jerk or self serving! Group members will be totally turned off by that and it may get you thrown out of the group.

Hosting Your Own Group

If you decide to host or manage your own Facebook Group or online community, be aware that managing and building it can be quite an investment of time and energy, maybe even hard dollar cost, depending on where you host your group. But it is a great way to keep engaged with your followers.

As with everything else, your own group must provide your members with one or more of the E-values that we talked about earlier: entertainment, education, enlightenment, or encouragement. What does that mean? Even though you're the leader, that doesn't give you license to spam your members with constant posts or messages that sell your books or other products! Sure, as a thank you for your service in leading the group, they'll tolerate one of your sales-y posts here or there. But the same 10 percent rule for book promotional posts applies here, too.

One of the other things I've done in my Facebook Group, and that I've also seen done in other well-run groups, is offer members occasional opportunities to post about themselves and their latest news. For example, on Tuesdays in my own Facebook group for authors, I do a post that launches a comment thread for members to make a comment with their latest accomplishments and promotions. As a leader I want to be a role model. So I post links to my books, blogs, and podcasts there, too. Much more subtle than if I would do a lot of separate "buy my stuff" posts.

Attending Events And Conferences

In-person and online events and conferences can be great places to bump into other people interested in your genre or topic, and to gain more understanding of your market.

I think you'll find, as I have, that announcements for every possible type of event pop up all over social media. This is another reason to get active in relevant Facebook Groups, online communities, and social media in general. Many events pay to advertise on social media, so you'll see a lot of events being promoted.

But there are some challenges for events.

Expense. Going to events and conferences can be pricey, depending on the event and market. Conferences I've run across in my market can cost up to hundreds of dollars or more, not including costs for travel or lodging. Even online events may have a cost.

Finding the Right Events and Conferences. This is

something that I've always found challenging, even for my small business networking. I've noticed that many event organizers have no clue about who their attendees really are, making it difficult to make a decision about investing in it.

For example, I've encountered many events that say they attract "small businesses." Yet they may only attract multilevel marketing representatives, real estate and insurance agents, financial advisors, and the like, all of whom could be nice people, but they have zero need for my books and services. I need events that attract lots of life and business coaches and consultants who are my primary targets.

Since you are investing in attending the events, contact the event organizer about the demographics of the attendees. If they're not willing or able to provide that information, you have to decide how much money you're willing to invest—or lose—by attending to check it out.

CHAPTER 4: YOUR AUTHOR ELEVATOR PITCH (OR SPEECH) FOR IN-PERSON NETWORKING

What should you say when you meet people? Authors who haven't done a lot of in-person networking may not know how to approach people. If this describes you, you'll need to script and practice what's called your elevator pitch, or elevator speech. The term elevator pitch comes from the days when entrepreneurs attempted to pitch potential investors during a skyscraper elevator ride of up to 60 seconds. That situation isn't as common these days due to security procedures and single-floor office buildings, but the term stuck.

Today, elevator pitches could be anywhere from 15 to 60 seconds. At some events I've attended, they gave the huge gathering of attendees just 5 seconds each to introduce themselves. You'll find that as the size of the attendee group goes up, the time allotted usually goes down to allow everyone a chance to speak within the event time limit. So you need to be ready to adjust your pitch. That takes preparation and practice.

If you only have a few seconds or so, try something that states your name, your genre or topic category, your latest book, and where to find it. When you have more time, you can expand on your basic short introduction pitch. Think of it as a building block. When I wrote ad copy for radio, my rule of thumb was 25 words per 15 seconds. That's a comfortable enough pace for most. And if you're given more time, add a detail or two about your book or you, again remembering that about 25 words fills up every 15-second block of time.

The Basic 15-Second Pitch Script

Here's the basic structure of a 15-Second Elevator Pitch for Authors:

"Hi, I'm [your name]. I write [your genre or topic category] for [type of reader]. My latest book, [title], is available on Amazon."

For me, this would sound like,

> *"Hi, I'm Heidi Thorne. I write books on sales and marketing for authors and speakers. My latest book, Understanding Your Creativity, is available on Amazon."*

(Side note: That's exactly 25 words.)

Note that this offers a call to action to find the book on Amazon. To facilitate their search, set up an author page on Amazon. It's free to get one through Amazon Author Central if you have a published book that's available on Amazon. That way, when someone searches for your name, your author page will show up in search results. You should have an Amazon author page whether you network or not since it provides a central place for people to learn more about you and your book, and offers them the opportunity to purchase it there, too.

"But I want them to buy my book from my website, Shopify, or my sales page on Lulu!" Okay, okay, I understand that you want to do that so you make more money per sale. But you have to remember that you want to make it as convenient and easy for people to remember you and your book from the few seconds they get to hear your pitch. They'll remember Amazon. You'll be lucky if they remember your name or your book title, even if they're interested. But if you insist on sending them to your non-Amazon site, make it an easy to remember URL.

Speaking of book titles in your elevator pitch, if your title is long, as many nonfiction titles are, abbreviate it. For example, one of my books is Understanding Your Creativity: Discover the Internal and External Factors that Affect Your Creative Life. I've probably lost them after the word "creativity." So I would just say that my book title is Understanding Your Creativity. Make it easy to remember you and your book.

CHAPTER 5: KEEPING FACE-TO-FACE INTRODUCTIONS AND CONVERSATIONS FROM GETTING WEIRD AND AWKWARD

What if you're meeting someone face-to-face for the first time? Essentially, you want to introduce yourself with a smooth segue into a conversation.

> *"Hi, I'm [your name]. I'm an author and I write [genre or topic category]."*

Again using myself as an example, I would say,

"Hi, I'm Heidi Thorne. I'm an author and I write business books to help small businesses and authors."

Then what do you say? Realize that people like to talk about themselves. The next thing out of your mouth should invite them to do so, so they won't feel bad about it. Depending on the event or group, here are some ideas for that question.

If no one is wearing name badges, say,

"I'm glad to meet you. What's your name and what kind of work do you do?"

If the person is wearing a name badge, say,

"I'm glad to meet you, [then say the name you see on the badge]. What kind of work do you do?"

A question like the one about work may have to change with the type of people you're meeting. If you know everyone at the event does a certain type of job, it's ignorant to ask what they do for work. But let's say you're all attending a national conference that most would have to travel to. You could change the follow-up question to:

"I'm glad to meet you, [then say the name you see on the badge]. Are you from this area or did you have to travel to get here?"

However they respond, listen for some clue about what to ask them next. For example, on the travel question, if you've been to where the person is from, you could ask him if he's enjoys a certain restaurant or popular destination in that area.

If and when the conversation turns to books, here's a question to get that rolling.

"Do you read a lot of books in [such-and-such genre or topic category]?"

The person's answer will tell you what path the conversation should follow next.

Scenario 1: If they answer yes to the genre question, then you can ask,

"What's your favorite book [or author] in [such-and-such genre or topic category], and what makes that your favorite?"

Notice, too, that I didn't suggest you ask, *"Why is that your favorite?"* A why question puts people on the defensive.

You're probably thinking, *"Why do I want them to talk about these other books? What about my book?"* Ego check! What you're doing here is getting them to talk about themselves and things that interest them which helps endear you to them. They'll think you're the smartest, coolest, nicest person there! Plus, you're doing market research to find out what's of interest to your target readers.

After they've talked about what they like, you can follow up with some comments about your favorite book and author in your genre or category, and that favorite should not be your book! Sometimes this will naturally lead to a longer conversation. That's nice, but you want to circulate around the event to meet more people. So you'll need to extract yourself from the conversation after maybe a minute or two. That way there's no pressure or rude exits for either party. Here's an example of what I mean when you get to a comfortable break point in the conversation.

"It's been wonderful talking with you. Thanks for your time. Here's my card. I hope you'll connect with me on social media. Enjoy the rest of the event."

Notice how you're inviting them to join you in further

connection and conversation, not buy your book. Building your author platform of fans is more important for your long term author success than a quick sale of one book.

Scenario 2: What if they say they don't read a lot of books like yours and aren't interested in you or your work? Actually, this situation will happen way more often than you'd like. What do you say then to keep it from getting uncomfortable and awkward?

First, you must understand that you are never, ever going to convert a disinterested person into a fan or a buyer. Never, ever! So don't prattle on about how your book will change their mind.

But you still may want to glean some marketing intel, and want to keep it positive, saying something like,

"That's okay. What type of books do you like to read?"

Again, the focus is on the reader, not you. You could then reply with whether you're a fan of those books, too, or follow up with,

"What makes that your favorite author [or type of book]?"

This can open up a friendly discussion. As before, you're trying to get market intel and you'll learn a lot from talking to real people face to face, even if they're not your core audience. Also, as before, you don't want to go on and on with any encounter. So when you've spent no more than a minute or two with the person, politely thank them for talking with you and move on with something like,

*"Thanks for taking a few moments to talk
with me. Enjoy the rest of the event."*

Notice that I didn't suggest you foist your business card on disinterested people, or even invite them to follow you on social media or elsewhere. They've already self-identi-fied as not being a potential fan. All you want from this dead end encounter is that they remember you as a nice au-thor person.

All this may sound and feel uncomfortable at first. But after practice and experience, you'll start to gain a sense of how to start and manage introductions and conversations. If you're totally new to in-person networking or are a complete introvert, role play with a close friend or family member before your next event so that you begin to think on your feet in a safe and friendly environment.

"So When Do I Sell Them A Book?"

At a recent networking event, one of the ladies at my table asked to see the copy of my latest book I had brought as "show and tell" for my 30-second introduction. She was interested in possibly buying it for a gift. Yay! So I gave her my card and told her the books were available on Amazon and Audible.

I could have made a quick sale that would have paid for my lunch and meeting fee. She also could have com-pletely forgotten about my book by the time she returned home. So selling it to her then would have prevented that sale from evaporating. Since I had the book with me, why didn't I sell it to her right then and there?

In this particular instance, the networking group pro-hibits attendees from making sales of products or ser-vices during the meeting and within the meeting facility altogether. A rule like this avoids creating an uncomfort-able situation for attendees who feel they'll be bombarded with sales pitches. So I didn't make the sale out of respect for the group's rules.

But even if it was allowed, I would still have just told her to buy it on Amazon. This avoids a lot of hassle for me in accepting payment, accounting for sales taxes, and more since Amazon handles it all for me.

I also don't want to look like a book peddler. I'm an author and leader of a tribe of fans! I don't think mega celebrity authors Stephen King and J.K. Rowling go to events with a bunch of books ready to sell to fans. So why should I? It hurts my author brand. Plus, when the interested person visits my author page on Amazon, they might see other books to buy.

Some networking groups may offer events or expos where you're given the opportunity to host an exhibit or sales table. There's usually a cost to host the table. That's the only scenario when going for the in-person direct-to-reader pitch to buy your book is appropriate. Just be careful with these opportunities since the cost to host a table might outweigh the potential book sales, and you'll lose money.

Selling On The Street?

An interesting scenario about approaching potential book buyers popped up in an authors group online. The author was wondering how to approach random people on the street about buying his book. Ugh! On the street? That'll have people screaming, *"Run away, run away!"*

Hitting up random people on the street—or anywhere! —about your book is cold calling. Though some aggressive salespeople will tell you otherwise, no one likes cold calling these days. No one, including both customers and sales-people.

But that's not the biggest problem with trying to sell your book to just anyone. The reason you're thinking about doing this is that you have no idea who your reader fans are. So you'll just take your chances by asking every human you encounter. It's just a numbers game. What a waste of energy and time that will brand you as desperate or a panhandler, and not the author star you are.

Sure, if you strike up conversations with strangers that lead to them asking about you and what you do, then it's appropriate to tell them about yourself and your book. As with networking events, don't trap these strangers into never-ending conversations. Follow the same rules as for a regular in-person networking conversation. Offer them your author business card. Then move on.

Will Fans Automatically Become Customers?

No. In networking, you're not going for the sale right then and there. You're looking to build your base of fans and fol-lowers that could become prospects for buying your book. The key word there is prospects. Just because they're fans of you and your work doesn't mean they'll automatically buy your book, although it increases the likelihood of a sale.

Fans have other ways to support you, even if they don't buy your book. They can follow and share your blog, podcast, and book announcements. They could facilitate introductions to people they know who could support you and your work. They can comment on your social media posts which may be just the feedback you were looking for.

Think less about the sale and more about gaining long-term support when it comes to building your network.

CHAPTER 6: YOUR AUTHOR NETWORKING TOOLS

Your Author Business Card

You've probably noticed that I mentioned your author business card earlier. I suggest that you have a very basic business card to offer new people that you meet in real life throughout your day and through networking.

What should you put on your author business card? Basic minimum information would include:

- **Your author name, or pen name.** If you use different pen names for different audiences and events, have a different card for each.

- **Your author website or blog.** Whichever you use as your primary author website.

Beyond that, you could add the following:

- **Primary social media networks you want them to follow you on... not every single one you're on!** For example, if you want them to follow you on your Facebook Business Page, use that.

- **Title of your latest book OR your Amazon author page.** If you have only one book, it's fine to include your book's title on your business card. But once you start self publishing lots of titles, it's too much. So you can just include your Amazon author page. That's what I do on my card because I have several book titles.

- **Email address?** Since I'm doing a fair amount of networking in business groups, I currently include my email address on my card. But I'm thinking about eliminating it for future cards since there are so many other ways to connect with me through my website or social media. Plus, I want them to visit my Amazon author page or website if they're interested in my books. I don't want them emailing me to buy, or waste my time by asking me for free advice.

- **Your photo.** Introverted authors won't like this one! I've found that including my photo on my cards helps people remember me. But if you're nervous about including your photo, or feel that it would present some security risk for you, don't include it!

What not to include?

- **Phone number.** Because I want to behave as a celebrity author, I am not including my phone number on my author business cards. I don't want random people calling me. I've also found that people will try to entangle you in nonsensical and irrelevant phone calls at the most inconvenient of times, usually because they want something from you or want to sell to you. I also cannot imagine a single instance where a reader would need to talk to me personally and immediately on the phone. Don't let random people disturb your life. Behave like an author superstar. I suggest leaving your personal phone number off your author business card, unless you have a business where you actually want people to call you on the phone.

Your Author Name Badge

Most business networking events will have some sort of name badge available for you to use. But a lot of Meetup groups, book clubs, and other more casual events often do not. So there's one more tool you'll need if you're planning to do a lot of in-person networking: A name badge. You might think that's silly. But I will tell you that from decades of attending networking events and trade shows, this is essential.

Wearing a name badge eliminates the awkward "What's your name?" questions and you can quickly get on to more useful conversation. Plus, they'll be seeing your name for the entire time you're speaking together so that they can more easily remember your name.

Get a high quality badge. Search for online sources for personalized name badges that you can use over and over again. These look more professional and can be used for years. Some badges have magnet back options so that you don't ruin your clothing with a pin back.

What should you put on your badge? Your name or pen name obviously. Then proudly put your job title of "Author" underneath your name. If you have space on the badge and want people to remember what you write, you could also add a line under your job title indicating what you write. Again, have different name badges if you use multiple pen names.

Don't hang a name badge on a lanyard because people will be staring at your chest or navel to read your name. Trust me, this happens. I can't think of anything more socially awkward than that. People are naturally looking to put a name with a face and not, well, any other part of your body. If the group or event requires you to wear the lanyard name tag for security purposes or whatever other reason, wear your regular name badge, too. It's not overkill. It's keeping your name where people will easily and comfortably see it. Speaking of keeping your name where people will see it, always wear your name badge near your shoulder area.

Bring A Print Copy Of Your Book

For in-person events, consider bringing a "show and tell" copy of your book's print edition to hold up during your 15-second elevator pitch. It helps you appear like a legit author, even if you primarily focus on your eBook or audio book sales.

If you don't plan to do big sales of a print edition, don't spend a fortune on this show copy of your book. Use a tool like Kindle Create from Kindle Direct Publishing to easily create a print on demand edition from your Kindle eBook file. And Kindle Create is a free tool. As I'm writing this, Kindle Create is still in beta mode, but it creates a print edition that's acceptable enough even now.

Alternatively, you could put a big image of your eBook or audio book cover on your mobile tablet-size device screen to show your book's cover during your elevator pitch. That's also a free way to create a show-and-tell display.

But don't whip out your book to show to each person you meet face to face. I have seen people do this with their books or other promotional materials many times over my years of networking. It makes you look like a pushy or insecure salesperson. It makes the other person feel uncomfortable, too, especially if they're not interested in your book. Wait until you can show your book to the entire group during your 15-second elevator pitch. Then put your display copy away.

True, some people may ask to see your display print book after the event and it's fine to show it to them if the group or event allows that. Stand right with the person who's looking at it so that you get it back. If they ask if they can buy one, tell them they can buy it on Amazon or wherever you're selling it.

Don't carry a bunch of your books to sell out of your bag or the trunk of your car. That's so bad for your professional author image! You look like you're selling your book at a flea market or garage sale. Remember that in networking, you're going for building your network of followers and fans, not just sales. How many garage sale and flea market sellers have loyal followers and fans? Not many, if any. I think you get my point.

CHAPTER 7: SPEAKING AT EVENTS AND CONFERENCES AS AN AUTHOR

In theory, speaking at events and conferences sounds like a great way to build awareness for yourself and your books. But like other opportunities I've discussed, there are some challenges.

Getting Speaking Gigs

This is the biggest problem! Many associations and community groups enlist speakers from their own membership. Events may also want recognized authors or celebrities. So it may take significant sales effort and outreach to even get considered as a speaker.

Be aware, too, that lots of groups, especially smaller local ones, may invite you to speak for free for "exposure." What they mean by that is that you will become recognized by their group because you're going to be featured as a speaker. Sometimes that truly is the case and it can benefit you. Other times, the group is just looking for someone, anyone, to fill a speaker vacancy and at no cost to them. Unless you're very inexperienced and introverted, and need to build your public speaking chops, don't accept every speaking invite, especially those that want you to speak for free.

Remember, too, that public speaking could have expenses such as for travel, as well as your time and energy. It can be exhausting. Trust me, I know. Only accept those gigs that help you reach your ideal reading audience and book promotion goals.

Avoiding The "Everyone Will Buy Your Book" Events

Another common speaking invitation authors receive is one that says, *"We can't pay you to speak, but you can sell your books at the back of the room. Everyone will want to buy your book!"* Maybe they will. More likely they won't. I've gotten stuck investing my time, energy, and even money to present at these events, only to sell literally one or two copies of my books and make no money after expenses. No, that's not true. I actually lost money.

Remember that selling books at an event is a complex affair. You have to have an inventory of books. If you normally sell your books as print on demand or electronic editions, this will be a cost to you to order up a supply of physical books. And if no one buys those print editions, you are stuck with the expense and inventory.

Plus, you'll have to have a way to process payments. More people are expecting to pay with credit cards. So you'll have to have a way to securely process those trans actions, usually on your mobile phone. That's another expense and hassle.

Then you have to mess with sales taxes. If this is news to you, you need to have a chat with your CPA or tax advisor to make sure you're handling this properly.

And you have to juggle all this while you might be trying to chat with attendees during a post-presentation meet and greet.

These days, I might have one display copy of each book I feature in my talk and a stack of my author business cards. If they're really interested, they'll buy later. And I really just want these attendees to join my network of fans on social media or elsewhere online. I'll do more intentional and direct selling to them once they've joined my author tribe.

Are You Really Networking? Or Are You The Show?

When you're the speaker, you're the star of the show. So attendees may treat you with deference or even some distance. That's not all bad since you are a leader of your fan tribe. The downside is that you might not make friendly, valuable connections to help build your author business. Have your author business card readily available so attendees will know where to follow you and buy your book, even if they don't get a chance to visit with you personally.

Building Your Email Subscriber List

Common business marketing advice up to now said that you should build your email subscriber list so you can keep in touch with your fans and market to them. Author speakers were inclined to take on even unpaid gigs just for the opportunity to build their email lists. But this is getting harder and harder as time goes on due to readers' information overload and privacy issues. Plus, open and click rates for email newsletters and promotions are declining over time because people just get too many emails.

Due to regulations such as CAN-SPAM and GDPR, collecting business cards or names and email addresses while networking, and automatically adding them to your email list, may no longer qualify as official opt-in permission. In fact, I'd recommend that if you don't have a formal, compliant, permission-based name and email collection system in place, it's probably better to suggest that attendees follow you on social media. Check with your reputable email broadcast provider—such as MailChimp, Constant Contact, or AWeber—for current compliant and best practice email address and personal information collection suggestions.

Decide what results you hope to achieve from speaking and carefully evaluate if the gig can deliver. Many can't. If you need some experience in public speaking, then accept more gig opportunities. But after that, if an event can't deliver connections to the right kind of readers, take a pass.

CHAPTER 8: SOCIAL MEDIA NETWORKING FOR AUTHORS

Being active on social media networks such as Facebook, Twitter, and LinkedIn can help build your tribe of fans efficiently and effectively. But don't be fooled into thinking it will be easy. It's difficult because most networks are now mature and very competitive. And the algorithm robots which run the networks are constantly changing how your posts are shown to fans and potential followers. That means it could take a long time to get people to follow and engage with you. It also means that the networks want you to spend on advertising to reach your ideal audience.

Realize, too, that these networks can change quickly, become irrelevant, or even disappear. Because of this constant state of flux, I'm even hesitant to offer any specific tips for specific networks. So I'll provide some general social media networking tips that should apply regardless of which networks are most popular when you read this.

Establish A Business Profile

Get started by establishing a business profile on social networks that you feel comfortable using. Notice that I said "business profile." On some networks, you can also use your personal profile for promotion of your work, while others prohibit it. Facebook, for example, requires you to set up a business page for promotional or business use. Even if you can use your personal profile for business, you may want to keep a separate profile for your author business.

Lurk And Experiment

Almost any social network can provide opportunities for you to build your fan base. The only way you'll discover which ones will be the best for you is by actually getting on the network, lurking, and experimenting. You won't know what works otherwise.

By lurking, I mean that you should follow and watch some relevant people in your market niche to see how they operate. How, what, and when do they post? Who follows them? Then start experimenting with posts of your own modeled after what seems to be working for them, of course, with your own special creative twist.

Be Genuine

Don't try to duplicate the posts of others. I've found that many popular accounts invest heavily in producing perfect photos, videos, and blogs that would be impossible for most individual self published authors to replicate. Do what you can with the resources and talents you have. Be yourself! People want to follow genuine people.

Follow The 10 Percent Rule

Social media users who are constantly creating "buy my stuff" posts are quickly ignored or outright unfollowed. Limit your "buy my book" and promotional posts to around 10 percent of your total posts. That's usually tolerable for most users.

Be Consistent

Limit the number of topics you cover in your social posting, focusing primarily on those that relate to your genre or topic. It doesn't hurt to throw in personal or fun posts to appear human and show your personality. But as with your book promotion posts, try to limit those off-topic posts so your followers don't get jumbled messages about you and your work.

Don't Expect Instant Results And Be Prepared For The Long Haul

Even though the duration of any post on a social network could be mere seconds, the time it takes to build a following could be months or years. Yes, years. So being consistent over a long period of time is critical to building momentum.

Engage To Get Engagement

Social media is a give-to-get proposition. You have to be posting content that provides at least one of the E-values for your followers: entertainment, education, enlighten-ment, or encouragement. I have seen so many authors con-stantly promoting their books on social. That's advertis-ing. No one wants to be bombarded with your promotions all the time. As noted earlier, keeping your promotional social media posts to about 10 percent of your total post-ing volume is usually tolerable.

Go Native, Monitor Your Results, And Adjust

As I'm writing this, most of the social networks have shifted their algorithms to favor showing posts that fea-ture content built on or for their particular network, also known as native content. So posts that include links to blogs and videos that are off the network may not be given much visibility to users. This can dramatically in-crease your social media investment. Every network has different nuances and requirements which means that you might have to create multiple versions of each post.

As well, this can reduce web traffic to your blogs or vid-eos, making it difficult to figure out what's really reson-ating with your fans. Your Google Analytics or other web traffic monitoring won't show much coming from social media to your site.

You may be able to get some insight from the analyt-ics reports on each network. Sometimes getting analytics will require you to set up a business account or profile on the social media network. For example, Facebook offers In-sights for business pages. It's probably worth setting up a business profile just to get a more accurate assessment of what's working.

Realize, too, that social media is a competitive and

noisy space. The constantly changing software algorithms that rule these networks are always changing, too. It can be very tough to get likes, shares, and new followers, and your actual numbers could be very low, especially for the first years. So don't get discouraged and watch for trends over time.

But when you see that a social media network is no longer producing desired realistic results for you after putting some effort in over time, you may need to make adjustments. You'll need to go back to experimenting mode to figure out if it's merely a change to your posts or posting schedule that's needed, or if you need to shift your efforts to a different network.

For a real life example, Twitter used to be my primary social network for years. But then as my market changed, and Twitter seemed to shift from conversation hub to news feed, I wasn't getting a lot of engagement, shares, and new followers. It was sad to see this happen since I had gained so many wonderful new friends and paying clients through Twitter in its early days.

In response to this trend, I upped my presence on Facebook and Instagram to test if they would be better for me. It turned out that they were. But that could change tomorrow, literally tomorrow.

Influencers Are Not Fans

One of the newer trends in social media marketing is influencers. Influencers are people on social media channels that have a relevant or sizable following of your ideal customers. Some people call them brand ambassadors. In the publishing arena, some may call them street teams or book launch teams.

Influencers can help get the word out on you and your work by posting about your books on their social profiles or blogs. Some will do this for a free review copy of the book. Others may charge you a fee. As I'm writing this, influencer marketing is still a developing marketing tactic.

Influencers may post as required for your deal with them, but they may not genuinely engage with your fans. Then once your deal with them is over, they're not obligated to continue engaging with your fans about you or your book. Influencers you hire are not technically part of your fan base. They may not follow you during or after your campaign, even though you're a paying client. While influencers can be part of your author network, they may or may not be your true fans. You've hired them, not inspired them, to promote you.

I have to admit that I'm not totally sold on self published authors hiring influencers for promoting their books. It's not that it's a bad idea in theory. It's just that at this point it requires a great deal of marketing skill, knowledge, and research to use this technique effectively. It is too unreliable and unstructured of a tactic for novice marketers like most self published authors. It's also a marketing tactic that is getting more scrutiny from agencies such as the Federal Trade Commission and IRS in the United States. Disclosures of your relationships with influencers are now being required by law, too.

Personally, I am not in favor of using book launch or street teams of influencers where you provide a free PDF copy of your book to a group of influencers. There is nothing to stop these people from sending this freebie to their entire email contact list, or they could even post a link to it on social media. Yikes! There go a ton of potential sales. Plus, who really believes that a ton of real customers would have had the time to read your book and post a review on the first day of your book launch?

According to Amazon's community and review guidelines as I wrote this, authors and publishers are allowed to provide free or discounted copies of books to readers. However, you cannot require a review on Amazon in exchange for the freebie. So engaging influencers for the purpose of getting them to post a review on Amazon may be in violation of Amazon policies. But if they post a review on their own blog, video, or social media channels, that appears to be okay, as long as they disclose they've received a copy for free.

An alternative is to offer a deeply discounted Kindle Countdown Deal or Kindle Free Book Promotion for a limited time during your book launch to encourage anyone, including influencers, to officially purchase the book and review. Better than having PDFs of your entire book floating all over the internet, or potentially violating Amazon guidelines.

A more economical and organic strategy is to create books that your true fans feel are worth reading and sharing with their own followers. Fan bases are built by one fan bringing another fan into the community. That takes time, but it will build a base that has the potential to support you well beyond the initial book launch.

CHAPTER 9: NETWORKING WITH OTHER AUTHORS

One group of readers that authors often ignore is other authors within their genre or topic. They tend to view them as competition, not colleagues and collaborators.

As an author, you read books, don't you? It's not like once you become an author, you quit reading books! Most authors are avid or rabid readers. So they can become a relevant, responsive, and supportive network for your work.

Remember, too, that you get to be a better writer by reading the work of other writers. I'm not just talking about reading the work of the superstar celebrity authors. Read the work of other self published authors in your market, too. You'll be better aware of the work that's available in your market, and how you and your work fit in that market.

Don't treat other authors like they're enemies stealing book sales from you. Follow them on social media. Make friendly and helpful comments on their social media posts, blogs, or videos to start conversations. Buy their books and leave constructive book reviews on Amazon or elsewhere. Invite them to buy, read, and review your books, too. These people understand your genre or topic and the writing challenges that go with it. So their feedback and support can be valuable.

With that in mind, I hope, as a fellow self published author, you'll join me on social media to continue the conversation we've started here. Visit my website at HeidiThorne.com for links, or just search for me on the major social networks.

ABOUT THE AUTHOR

Heidi Thorne

Hi, I'm Dr. Heidi Thorne, MBA/DBA, a nonfiction book editor and author. Prior to pursuing my writing career, I was a trade newspaper editor for over 15 years, taught at the college level for five years, and had a long career in sales and advertising. In my books, blog, and online resources, I share my publishing and marketing experience to help authors like you avoid embarrassing and expensive mistakes when self publishing.

I also invite you to check out my podcast, The Heidi Thorne Show, where I discuss self publishing. You can listen and subscribe to the show on major podcast platforms including Apple Podcasts, Spotify, Stitcher, and YouTube.

My books are available on Amazon, Audible, and Apple Books. Search for my name on those sites for a list of currently available titles on my author page.

To connect with me, visit my website at HeidiThorne.com.

9 798609 753014